Even in the Silence

Finding Joy in the Waiting

❦

Famia Green

Author of Becoming a Joy Warrior

Published by Joy Warrior Press
www.thejoypursuitjourney.com

Dedication

To my Children,
Who became the living chapters of this message.
Through you, God revealed what it means to hold joy through every
season and to keep faith anchored when storms come our way.

Even When

"I believe in the sun,
Even when it is not shining.
I believe in love,
Even when I don't feel it.
I believe in God
Even when He is silent.
(A poem found on a cellar wall during the
Holocaust)

A Note from
My Heart Before We Begin

Waiting has marked most of my life. Sometimes for short seasons, many times it lasted for years. I have a strong instinct to solve problems and take control. There was very little I could fix or hold together. Some parts of my life felt broken. I prayed and asked God to make it right. I wanted movement and relief. I wanted God to hurry His plan.

He responded simply, "Wait and trust me." He reminded me answers would come in His time, not mine.

Waiting teaches us in ways we don't expect. It exposes longing and reveals what we reach for when fear rises. It shows what we believe about God when discouragement presses in. God asked me to trust Him at a time when my faith felt weak and I couldn't see anything coming my way.

Long stretches of silence pressed on my heart. I sat with grief and confusion. Storms rose without warning, and I felt tossed by the waves. In those moments, I sensed the Lord ask "Where are you looking?" Well, I couldn't help but look at the waves that were tossing me about.

He said, "Lift your head and look at me. Don't look at the waves, look to the horizon where I stand. I lead you forward one step at a time."

I am learning to follow and trust that He will make all things work out. My faith is not perfect. I still struggle, yet I know the Lord holds all the answers and has a plan for our lives. I only need to reach out to Him and spend time in His presence, and a peace washes over me. I can rejoice again because I have taken my eyes off the problems and onto Him. I have to make the effort to do this and trust His promises over my life and over the lives of those I love.

This book came from those long years of learning what He taught me.

I am walking this road, and I am grateful to walk beside you. Step by step we will look toward the horizon together, come take my hand. Let us begin this journey of learning to practice joy in the waiting.

How to Use This Book

This devotional journal invites you to move at your own pace and pause where God speaks. It is a space to meet with the Lord, the One who sees you, knows what you are waiting for, and walks you through it

Each day includes:

- **Scripture**

  A guiding verse or verses to reflect on.

- **Devotional**

  A story, teaching, or reflection to guide you deeper into trusting God in the waiting.

- **His Voice in the Waiting**

  This is a moment to rest and receive encouragement from God's heart. Let them remind you that He is near and faithful.

- **Faith in Motion**

  A simple action or next step to live what you are learning.

- **Scripture in Action**

  Reflect on how God's Word is at work in your life. You'll be invited to journal, rewrite a verse as a declaration, or remember His faithfulness in your story.

- **Pause & Ponder**

  Questions to help you reflect, listen, and process what God is stirring in your heart.

- **Joy Spark**

  A small, intentional practice that helps you notice joy and beauty in every day.

- **Closing Prayer**

  A short prayer to surrender the day and rest in God's presence.

Table Of Contents

CHAPTER 1

Breaking Through

Scripture

"See, I am doing a new thing. Now it springs up; do you not perceive it? I am making a way in the wilderness and streams in the wasteland." Isaiah 43:19

"But, those who wait upon the Lord shall renew their strength; they shall mount up with wings like eagles, they shall run and not be weary; they shall walk and not faint." Isaiah 40:31

Devotional

In the early days of spring, long before the wind softens and the sun begins to linger, the daffodil rises.

The ground is frozen and the soil is firm. There is no evidence that winter is finished. Still, this flower pushes upward. Something unseen moves beneath the surface, reaching toward a promise not yet fulfilled.

The daffodil does not wait for permission. It does not ask for proof that the season is safe. It responds to the life-giving power placed deep within its design, the same power God placed in us. The strength to break through lives within us. When we fix our eyes on the frozen ground, we forget that it is God who causes us to rise and not ourselves.

Maybe you've prayed, believed, and stayed faithful, and yet you see no movement. Like the daffodil, something deeper is happening beneath the surface. You are not forgotten. God is not finished, and the silence does not mean God is absent. The daffodil knows its purpose. It knows when the time is right, it will push through the dark soil and bring hope that spring is near. In the same way, God has planted a purpose in you, a plan shaped by His hands. Scripture reminds us that we are God's workmanship, created in Christ Jesus for a purpose He prepared long before we could see it. You may not see it yet, but it's growing even in the silence. In Isaiah 43:19 God declares that He is doing a new thing, even when we don't perceive it. This verse isn't a call to look harder; it's an invitation to trust deeper.

The Hebrew root for "perceive" means to know through relationship. God is not asking us to see with our eyes. He invites us to believe with our hearts and stay connected to Him, even when the surface looks barren. When we do, faith begins to take root where sight cannot. Breakthrough starts beneath the soil long before it ever reaches the light.

His Voice in the Waiting

I planted you with purpose.
Even here, in the silence, I am at work.
You don't have to understand it all.
Stay connected to Me.

Faith in Motion

Choose one small act of obedience today, a step that feels like a stretch but points toward growth. It might be opening your Bible again, calling a friend, or simply whispering a prayer: "God, I trust You even here."

Scripture in Action:

"But, those who wait upon the Lord shall renew their strength; they shall mount up with wings like eagles, they shall run and not be weary; they shall walk and not faint." Isaiah 40:31

- What feels dormant in your life right now?
- Where do you sense God inviting you to stay connected even when you don't see change?

- Choose one verse that spoke to you recently. Rewrite it in your own words as a personal declaration.

Pause + Ponder

- Where has fear kept you captive?
- How do you sense God meeting you in this place of waiting?
- What truth brings comfort as you trust Him here?

Joy Spark

Look for signs of growth today. Not everything blooms at once, notice signs of movement. A kind word spoken. A breath of peace. A moment of courage. These are reminders that joy is still breaking through.

Closing Prayer

God, when the ground around me feels frozen and silent,

remind me that You are the God of new beginnings.

Help me stay rooted in You, even when I don't see the fruit yet.

Thank You for planting purpose in me and for growing something

beautiful through every waiting season. I choose to trust You today.

In Jesus' name,

Amen.

God isn't asking us to see with our eyes. He invites us to believe with our hearts and stay connected to Him, even when the surface looks barren.

Notes

_____

_____

_____

_____

_____

_____

_____

_____

_____

_____

_____

_____

_____

_____

_____

_____

_____

_____

_____

_____

_____

_____

_____

CHAPTER 2

The Ache of Unanswered Prayer

Scripture

"Why, my soul, are you downcast? Why so disturbed within me? Put your hope in God, for I will yet praise him, my Savior and my God." Psalm 42:5

"Those who wait on the Lord will renew their strength. They will soar on wings like eagles; they will run and not grow weary; they will walk and not faint." Isaiah 40:31

"Though the fig tree does not bud and there are no grapes on the vines... yet I will rejoice in the Lord, I will be joyful in God my Savior." Habakkuk 3:17–18

Devotional

The ache of unanswered prayer reaches deeper than disappointment. It presses into the soul, raising questions that words cannot quiet. "Lord, do You hear me?" "Why isn't anything changing?" "How long must I wait?" You pray with persistence. You cry through the night. You ask for direction, yet each request hung in the air without reply.

The psalmist knew this ache: "Why, my soul, are you downcast? Why so disturbed within me?" His words reveal a heart that feels the weight of heaven's stillness. They are raw and unpolished. They show us that God does not turn away from honest lament.

In the same breath, the psalmist speaks hope: "I will yet praise him, my Savior and my God." This declaration does not erase the ache. It names God as faithful in the middle of the waiting. Praise becomes an anchor for us when our prayers are unanswered.

We all carry this tension. A prayer for healing that lingers unanswered. A plea for reconciliation that stretches across a widening gap. A request for provision waits with empty hands. These moments shake the ground beneath our feet. They expose where we are placing our trust. Do we cling to outcomes, or to God?

The psalmist refuses to hide his struggle. He names his discouragement. "Why, my soul, are you downcast?" The word downcast paints the picture of a soul bent low under the weight of sorrow. His heart aches. His spirit was unsettled, his hope dimmed. He does not mask the pain with a smile or a shallow word of encouragement. He speaks the truth about what he feels.

This honesty is itself an act of faith. To bring the raw ache before God is to trust that He can carry it. God never asks us to pretend. He invites us to bring our real questions, our deep griefs, and our unmet desires into His presence.

The psalmist then shifts his focus. After naming the ache, he speaks to his own soul: "Put your hope in God." This is a command, not a suggestion. He is preaching to himself. His emotions cry out one story, but he calls his soul to rest in another. Hope is not tied to an outcome. It is tied to God Himself.

Notice the future tense in his words: "I will yet praise him." The answer has not arrived. The silence has not lifted. The prayer remains unanswered. Still, he declares that praise is coming. This is not denial of the present; it is confidence in the faithfulness of God.

The word yet becomes a hinge in the verse. Everything before it is weighed down by despair. Everything after it rises with hope. Isaiah speaks to those who wait. He does not promise quick answers. He promises strength. Waiting on the Lord is not wasted time. It becomes the ground where God renews weary hearts. He replaces striving with endurance as we keep our eyes on Him. In His presence, weariness gives way to strength, and hopelessness yields to joy.

Habakkuk looked at fields without crops, the vines without fruit, and the pens without livestock. Nothing around him gave reason for hope. Yet he declared, "I will rejoice in the Lord. I will be joyful in God my Savior." His joy rose from trust in God's character. He didn't need to see the evidence before rejoicing.

Unanswered prayer doesn't prove God's absence. It becomes the place where faith matures. It teaches us to praise without proof and trust without sight. In the ache of waiting, God invites us to believe by faith He will fulfill His word. If we need proof, we are no longer operating in faith.

His Voice in the Waiting

I hear your prayers even when you think they go unnoticed. My silence is not distance. I am closer than you realize. I see the tears you cry in secret. I know the weight you carry. Rest in Me and trust that I am working in ways you cannot see. My timing is not slow, and my promises will not fail. I am your refuge and your strength, your ever-present help. Stay near to Me, and you will find that I am closer than you think.

Faith in Motion

Choose one prayer request that feels unanswered and place it before God in a new way today. Instead of repeating the request, begin by thanking Him for who He is. Thank Him for His faithfulness, for His goodness, for His presence, in your life. Let your focus shift from the outcome you long for to the character of the God you trust.

If you have carried the same request for weeks, months, or even years, write it down on a separate sheet of paper. After you write it, fold it and set it aside in your Bible or journal. Each time you open your Bible, let that folded page remind you that you have placed it in God's hands. This action does not erase the ache; it becomes a daily reminder that the burden no longer rests on your shoulders.

Faith in motion often looks like surrender. Surrender means active trust, not passivity. It chooses to believe that God is at work even when you cannot see the evidence. Your step today may feel small, every time you shift your eyes from the silence to the Lord, you practice the faith that carries you forward.

Scripture in Action

"Why, my soul, are you downcast? Why so disturbed within me? Put your hope in God, for I will yet praise him, my Savior and my God." Psalm 42:5

When you face the ache of unanswered prayer, Psalm 42:5 gives you a pattern to follow:

- Name the pain. Be honest about the heaviness in your heart. God is not threatened by your questions.

- Preach to your soul. Speak truth into the silence. Tell your own heart where to place its hope.

- Declare future praise. Even when you see no change, decide in advance that God will receive your worship.

The ache of unanswered prayer is real. The psalmist does not minimize it, neither should we. In the middle of that ache, we hold this truth: God remains our Savior and our God. Hope in Him will never be wasted.

Pause + Ponder

Take a quiet moment to breathe in the truth you read. Let it settle in your heart before you begin.

- Bring one unanswered prayer to your journal. Name the ache with honesty and allow your heart to speak without holding back.

- As you sit with this ache in God's presence, what rises within you? Write the thoughts and emotions that surface as you wait with Him.

- How might choosing to worship in advance, saying "I will yet praise Him" shift the way you face unanswered prayer right now?

Joy Spark

Write the word YET in large letters on a page in your journal or on a card you can place somewhere visible. Decorate it, color it in, or frame it with designs that remind you of life and hope. Each time you see that word today, let it remind you that even when prayers are unanswered, God is still faithful. Speak it aloud: "I will yet praise Him."

This simple word, yet, can shift the atmosphere of your heart. It pulls your focus from what feels silent to the God who never stops working.

Closing Prayer

Lord, I bring before You the ache of prayers that feel unanswered.

You know the cries of my heart even when words run dry.

Teach me to trust You when silence surrounds me.

Help me speak truth to my soul, to anchor my hope in You,

and to choose praise even when I cannot see the outcome.

Draw me close in the waiting, and remind me that You remain my Savior and my God.

In Jesus' Name,

Amen

In the ache of waiting, God invites us to believe by faith that He will fulfill His Word. If we need proof, we are no longer operating in faith.

Notes

CHAPTER 3

When Striving Ceases

Scripture

"Be still, and know that I am God."

Psalm 46:10

"Let all that I am wait quietly before God, for my hope is in Him.

Psalm 62:5

Devotional

Some battles are not won by doing more.

Some are won by surrender.

In a world that applauds hustle and praises productivity, it can feel unnatural, maybe even irresponsible, to stop striving. We measure our worth by checklists and accomplishments. When life feels uncertain, we default to doing, fixing, solving, and trying harder.

What if stillness is not passive?

What if God invites us to trust Him by releasing the illusion of control?

Psalm 46 paints a picture of chaos: "Nations are in uproar, kingdoms fall; He lifts his voice, the earth melts". The earth gives way, the mountains fall into the sea, and its waters roar and foam. Right in the middle of that unrest comes a holy interruption: "Be still, and know that I am God."

Stillness is not silence for the sake of silence. It is not apathy or laziness. It is an intentional pause in the middle of the noise, a bold declaration that God remains sovereign even when the world shakes around us. When you feel like you have to keep moving to survive, stillness becomes an act of war against fear.

We may not like the quiet. It can expose all the thoughts we have pushed down and all the anxieties we have tried to outrun. Stillness also makes room for peace. It opens the door for His voice to quiet us. It reminds us that the outcome is not in our hands.

This kind of trust is not built overnight. It is cultivated in the waiting. God does some of His most transformative work when we pause and recognize that He is God, our Shepherd, and we are His sheep. The sheep follow the Shepherd because He knows the way, and they trust His voice.

Strength rises when striving ceases. It is the kind of strength that says, "I don't have to figure this out. I can rest in Him. When we stop wrestling for control and start resting in His presence, we find peace.

Stillness is not passive. The Hebrew word used in Psalm 46:10 is often translated "be still," but it carries a deeper meaning, one that invites us to cease striving, to let go, and to release our grip on what we were never meant to control. It is not a gentle suggestion to quiet our surroundings. It is a holy command to lay down our weapons, both physical and emotional, and to trust that the battle belongs to the Lord.

God is calling us to surrender what we have been clinging to in fear. That might be the outcome we are trying to control, the approval we are desperate to gain, or the constant pressure to hold everything together. Stillness says, "I don't need to carry this anymore." It creates space for God to carry what we cannot.

When we are still, our perspective begins to shift. We stop obsessing over the worst-case scenario and start remembering the faithfulness of God, who has never failed us. Stillness is not about zoning out or numbing our emotions. It is about re-centering our gaze. Our focus moves away from what feels uncertain and back to what is unchanging: God's presence, His power, and His peace.

Sometimes this stillness comes in literal silence. A quiet room. A paused moment in a hectic day. Other times, stillness happens within. Even when the world is noisy, we can cultivate an inner calm rooted in the knowledge that God is still God, and He is with us. It's like those people who fall asleep on the subway, untouched by the noise around them. That's what true stillness is, peace that rests in the presence of God no matter where we are.

Worship can be a part of this, though not in the performance sense. True worship is a posture of the heart. It is the surrender that says, "You are God, and I am not." In the stillness, worship does not always sound like singing. It may look like breathing deeply, sitting in Scripture, or choosing trust when our minds want to spiral. These quiet acts of surrender are worship too. Worship can also be playing praise songs and dancing around the house.

Stillness invites us to stop striving, to release our grip on control, and to remember who God is. This verse calls us to acknowledge His sovereignty, to trust His presence, and to rest in the assurance He is working even when we cannot see it. Stillness shifts our focus from our own effort to God's authority. When we quiet our hearts before Him, we discover hope in hardship, strength in surrender, and peace in knowing that He is our refuge.

His Voice in the Waiting

Let go of the list,
the pace,
the pressure.
Come sit awhile.
You don't have to run to be seen.
You don't have to strive to be held.
You don't have to win the war.
Be still and remember who fights for you.

Faith in Motion

Take ten minutes to practice stillness. Set a timer if
needed. No music, no phone, and no journaling. Sit
in the presence of God. Breathe deeply. When
distractions come, let them pass. Whisper His name
and stay awhile. Let stillness become your sanctuary.

Scripture in Action:

Reflect:

- Reflect on Psalm 62:5. What would it look like for all that you are, your thoughts, emotions, and plans, to wait quietly before the Lord today?
- What keeps you from resting in Him?
- Write a short declaration of hope, beginning with, "My hope is in God, even when..."

Joy Spark

Notice something today you would have missed if you had kept rushing. It might be sunlight falling across the floor, the sound of your own breath, or a Scripture that settles in at the right time. Maybe it's the color of leaves changing at the edge of fall, the smile of a child, or the welcome of a dog when you walk through the door. Let yourself notice these small gifts; they are glimpses of joy meant to remind you that God is near.

Closing Prayer

Lord, I surrender the parts of me that try to prove,
perform, or push my way
through uncertainty.
Teach me how to still my heart.
Anchor me in the truth that You are God
and I am safe in Your hands.
Help me release the grip of striving
and receive the gift of Your peace.
In Jesus' Name,
Amen

In stillness, we stop striving, release our grip on control, and remember who God is.

Notes

_____

_____

_____

_____

_____

_____

_____

_____

_____

_____

_____

_____

_____

_____

_____

_____

_____

_____

_____

CHAPTER 4

Where Faith Keeps Knocking

Scripture

"Ask and it will be given to you; seek and you will find; knock and the door will be opened to you. For everyone who asks receives; the one who seeks finds; and to the one who knocks, the door will be opened." Matthew 7:7–8

"If you remain in Me and My words remain in you, ask whatever you wish, and it will be done for you." John 15:7

"This is the confidence we have in approaching God: that if we ask anything according to His will, He hears us. And if we know that he hears us—whatever we ask—we know that we have what we asked of him." 1 John 5:14–15

Devotional

Prayer often feels like knocking on a closed door. You place your request before God and wait for movement on the other side. At times the waiting grows long. You wonder if anyone hears your knocking or if your prayers are reaching beyond the ceiling.

Jesus gives us a picture of prayer that is persistent: ask, seek, knock. The words are active and ongoing. They invite us not to give up after one prayer but to keep coming back. To keep asking. To keep seeking. To keep knocking. Prayer is not about persuading God to care. It is about staying in His presence long enough for Him to shape our hearts.

When we keep knocking, we are practicing trust. Every prayer becomes another declaration that God is the one with the power to open the right doors. Every request laid before Him reminds us that He is our Father, and we are His children dependent on His hand for strength and provision.

The ache of unanswered prayer can make us want to pull our hand away from the door. Discouragement whispers, stop knocking. Nothing will change. Fear suggests God has forgotten you. Yet Jesus urges us to keep knocking with confidence, because our Father gives good gifts to his children. He does not withhold what we need.

Hannah's life shows us what it means to keep knocking. Year after year, she carried the ache of unanswered prayer for a child (1 Samuel 1). Her sorrow pressed heavy on her soul, her waiting tested her faith, and her prayers fell into a deep well of silence. Yet she did not stop coming before the Lord. She poured out her soul at the temple, her anguish spilling over so much that Eli mistook her grief for drunkenness. Her persistence was not polished or perfect. It was raw, tear-filled, and desperate. Still, she kept knocking.

In time, God opened Hannah's womb, and she gave birth to Samuel, a child she dedicated back to the Lord. Her story reminds us that waiting does not mean abandonment. It shows us that God honors the cries of a heart that refuses to stop knocking, even when the years stretch out.

Like Hannah, we may not see immediate answers. We may feel misunderstood or weary. Yet her faith teaches us that the God who hears our cries is faithful. He sees, He remembers, and in His timing he responds.

Faith that keeps knocking is faith that refuses to let go of God's character. It rests on the assurance that He hears, He knows, and He gives what is best in His timing.

His Voice in the Waiting

I hear your knock.
Every prayer you bring to me reaches my heart.
Don't grow weary when the doors are closed.
I am teaching you to trust My timing.
I give good gifts, and I will not withhold what you need.
Keep asking, and you will see my faithfulness.
Keep seeking, and you will find that I am near.
Keep knocking, and you will learn that I open doors no one can shut.

Faith in Motion

Take a page in your journal and draw a simple door. Inside the outline, write one prayer you continue to bring before God. Around the doorframe, list moments when God has answered you in the past. Each time you look at it, let it remind you that the God who opened doors before will open the right one again.

Write your core request in one sentence. Keep it simple and focused.

List one step of obedience you can take this week that aligns with that request.

Choose a daily time to return to the door in prayer. Protect that time as sacred.

Every knock matters. Each prayer builds perseverance in your faith.

Scripture in Action

"Ask and it will be given to you; seek and you will find; knock and the door will be opened to you. For everyone who asks receives; the one who seeks finds; and to the one who knocks, the door will be opened." Matthew 7:7–8

Confidence in prayer does not come from perfect words or strong feelings. It comes from knowing that the Father listens and responds with wisdom.

The door may not open the way you expect, but the promise stands. He hears you, and He will act.

Every knock matters. Every prayer reaches Him.

Our confidence rests in the Father who holds the keys.

Today:

Bring one request to God again, and pray,

"Father, You hear me. I trust Your timing."

Pause + Ponder

- What fear tries to pull your hand away from the door?

- Where do you see your request beginning to align with Jesus' words?

- What door has God opened for you in the past that strengthens your faith today?

- How would your prayers change if you believed every knock reached His heart?

- What part of Hannah's story encourages you most in your own waiting?

Joy Spark

Notice the doors that God has already opened for you. They might be opportunities, healed relationships, or answers to old prayers. Let each one remind you, the same God who opened those doors before is still working today, preparing the right one to open again.

Closing Prayer

Father, I come again.
You invite me to keep on knocking,
so today I am knocking again.
Lord, set my heart to abide in Your Son.
Shape my request to align with Your will.
Give me strength to keep asking, seeking, and knocking.
Guard my mind with your peace.
Help me to grow joy in the waiting.
I place my timeline in your hands.
I trust your heart.
In Jesus Name,
Amen.

When we keep knocking, we are practicing trust. Every prayer becomes a declaration that God is the one with the power to open the right door.

Notes

CHAPTER 5

Choosing Joy in the Waiting

Scripture

"I remain confident of this: I will see the goodness of the Lord in the land of the living. Wait for the Lord; be strong and take heart and wait for the Lord."

Psalm 27:13–14

Devotional

Waiting is one of the hardest seasons to walk through. It feels like standing in the in-between, suspended between what God has promised and what has yet to come. Our hearts ache for resolution, our prayers circle around the same request, and our souls wrestle with silence.

The psalmist does not ignore the reality of fear or delay. He calls us to courage: "Wait for the Lord; be strong and take heart, wait for the Lord."

The temptation in waiting is to give up hope or to believe God has forgotten us. Yet waiting is not wasted time. Scripture shows us again and again that waiting is often the place where God's deepest work happens.

Abraham and Sarah also waited. Twenty-five years passed between God's promise of a son and the birth of Isaac. Their waiting tested their faith and revealed their humanity, yet it also displayed God's power to do the impossible. In their story we see that joy grows when we place our confidence in God who keeps His promises.

Jacob's love for Rachel led him to serve his father in-law for 14 years. Those years were long, his perseverance showed the depth of his devotion. His story teaches us that joy can grow even in the discipline of waiting.

The Israelites endured four hundred years of slavery before God delivered them through Moses. Their cries reached heaven, and though deliverance did not come quickly, God's rescue was certain. Their story points us to a God who hears even when the wait feels unbearable.

Even Jesus waited. For more than thirty years He lived in obscurity before His public ministry began. The Son of God knew the weight of waiting, and in His waiting, God was preparing the world for salvation.

As great a relationship as Paul had with God, he waited. He prayed consistently that God would heal the thorn in his flesh. He waited in prison. He waited to travel to countries he longed to evangelize. His life in prison was all about waiting, yet he found joy in accepting whatever the Lord gave him and chose to focus only on the good.

He worshiped while he waited. He strengthened the churches by sending letters of encouragement and correction while sitting in a dark cold prison chained to guards. He stayed rooted in joy and encouraged believers across generations to hold fast through every season

These stories remind us that God weaves purpose into every season of waiting. While we wait, He continues writing our story. His timing rarely matches ours. He always works on our behalf. He prepares, shapes, and strengthens us for what's ahead.

Joy in the waiting doesn't come through quick answers. It grows as you trust the God who holds the timeline. Philippians 4:4 calls us to rejoice in the Lord always. This means we rejoice when prayers are answered and also while we are waiting.

Joy does not deny the ache; it rests in the assurance of God's presence. In the waiting room of life, joy stands and declares, I worship, I trust, I hope.

Waiting reflects active trust, setting our hearts on God's character instead of our circumstances. It shows a faith that believes that His goodness will break through in His time. Abraham and Sarah learned that nothing is too hard for the Lord. that waiting is not abandonment; it is preparation.

His Voice in the Waiting

I hear every prayer you bring. I hold every tear you release in faith.

My timing is not your timing, yet My timing is perfect.

Joy does not wait for the answer to appear.

You can choose joy now as you wait on Me.

Let your hope grow strong in My presence.

Trust that I will guide you, strengthen you, and lead you in the right moment.

I am working while you wait.

Stay near me. I am your Shepherd and I will lead you.

Faith in Motion

- Write out your core prayer, pouring out your heart before the Lord.

- Choose one worship song to sing while you wait, declaring joy before the answer comes.

- Write down the moments when God has been faithful in your life. Keep that list nearby for days when hope feels weak.

Scripture in Action

"I remain confident of this: I will see the goodness of the Lord in the land of the living. Wait for the Lord; be strong and take heart and wait for the Lord."

Psalm 27:13–14

Waiting is not wasted. God promises that we will see His goodness in the land of the living. Which means we will see His hand at work while we are alive. Even when the answers feel delayed, His goodness will break through in His timing.

God's goodness means He moves toward you with love, not away from you in silence. It is His steady care for your life, guiding, protecting, strengthening, and providing in ways seen and unseen. His goodness means He can be trusted to work for your good even in seasons that feel heavy or slow.

It is a place where trust grows and joy takes root.

Today:

Bring your longing to God knowing that He hears you.

Say: "Lord, I wait in hope. You will guide me in Your time."

Pause + Ponder

- What prayer have you been carrying into God's presence again and again?
- Which biblical story of waiting speaks most to your heart right now, and why?
- Where have you seen glimpses of God's goodness even before the full answer came?

Joy Spark

Joy grows in the smallest moments of waiting. Light a candle as you pray and let its steady flame remind you of God's presence. Step outside and notice one glimpse of beauty in creation: a bird's song, a flower pushing through the soil, or the evening sky painted with color. Write down one thing you are grateful for today, even in the middle of delay. Each act of gratitude becomes a seed of joy planted in the waiting.

Closing Prayer

Father, I choose to wait on You with courage.

Give me strength when my heart feels weary.

Teach me to rejoice in You while I wait, to trust Your timing,

and to see Your goodness even in delay. Shape me in the waiting,

and let my hope rise in Your faithfulness.

I place my timeline in Your hands. I choose joy while I wait.

In Jesus' Name,

Amen

Waiting is not wasted time. It is often the place where God does His deepest work.

Notes

CHAPTER 6

Learning to Hope Again

Scripture

"May the God of hope fill you with all joy and peace as you trust in Him, so that you may overflow with hope by the power of the Holy Spirit." Romans 15:13

"For God alone, my soul waits in silence, for my hope is in Him". Psalm 62:5

Devotional

Disappointment has a way of closing the heart. When prayers linger unanswered or life unravels in ways we never expected, hope feels too risky. It's easier to guard ourselves, to stop expecting good things, and to lower the bar so we don't get let down again.

God calls us to a different way. He does not ask us to pretend everything is fine. He invites us to open our hearts again and learn how to hope. True hope is not wishful thinking. It is confidence rooted in the character of God.

Psalm 62:5 was written by David, while he was facing opposition from every side. Words of accusation and discouragement surrounded him. Yet in the middle of it all, he spoke to his own soul and chose to rest in God. His hope did not rest in circumstances or in people changing. His hope rested in God alone. God had been faithful before, and David believed He would be faithful again.

We all know what it feels like to be disappointed again and again. You prayed and nothing changed. You believed and the answer did not come. In those moments, hope fades, and despair starts to settle in our hearts. Yet God still reaches out to us and asks us to lift our eyes to Him again.

Even when David was in the depths of despair, he reminded himself to praise God, who ultimately had a plan for his life. David understood how quickly hope can fade when his eyes stayed on the battle. He turned his gaze to God, finding strength again in His faithfulness. Remembering who God is becomes the doorway to renewed hope. We face the same struggle. Our hope wavers when we stare at the weight of our circumstances. God calls us to lift our heads and focus our eyes on Him. Redirecting our gaze renews our minds and lifts the weight from our shoulders.

Romans 15:13 is both a prayer and a promise. Paul reminds us that God Himself is the source of hope. Hope grows from trust. Trust plans the seed, and hope begins to grow from that place. When we rely on God, hope expands in us and overflows touching everything in our lives.

That kind of hope carries us through seasons of silence and delay. It reminds us that God is working even when we can't see movement. It strengthens us to take the next step, even when the future feels uncertain.

To hope again is to believe that God is still writing your story. It is to trust that what looks delayed is not denied. It is to allow the Spirit to breathe courage back into your heart.

His Voice in the Waiting

I know that waiting stretches your heart. I am here by your side,
Encouraging you to trust that I have a plan for you.
Waiting with hope means believing that I am still writing your story.
Let me fill your heart with peace and strength as you wait.
I am working, even when you cannot see it. Stay close to Me,
And hope will grow again.

Faith in Motion

- Write out Psalm 62:5 on a card and keep it where you will see it often. Speak it aloud when discouragement rises, choosing to hope again.

- Begin a "Hope Journal." Each day, record one way you saw God's presence or provision.

- Share one place of discouragement with a trusted friend or prayer partner. Invite them to believe with you.

- Choose a worship song that declares God's faithfulness and sing it as an act of hope.

Scripture in Action

"May the God of hope fill you with all joy and peace as you trust in Him, so that you may overflow with hope by the power of the Holy Spirit." Romans 15:13

- Read Romans 15:13 slowly. Sit with each phrase and let its words settle over your heart.

- Rewrite the verse using your own name, turning it into a personal prayer.

- What part of your heart needs God to restore hope again?

Pause + Ponder

- Where have you stopped hoping because of disappointment?
- What memory of God's faithfulness can fuel hope today?
- How does it change your heart to see God as the source of hope?
- What step of faith can you take this week to open your heart to hope again?

Joy Spark

Seasons change, and with them come small signs of wonder. Look for one today, changing leaves, a sunrise or sunset, a beautiful rainbow, flower pushing up in unlikely places, talking with friends, neighbors or God.

Notice them as you go, so you begin to see joy all around you.

Closing Prayer

God of hope, pour joy into my weary heart.
Flood me with peace as I trust you.
Teach me to place my hope in you,
not in what I see.
When disappointment tries to close my heart,
remind me of your faithfulness.
In Jesus' Name,
Amen

To hope again is to believe that God is still writing your story.

Notes

CHAPTER 7

Strength for the Journey

Scripture

"Blessed are those whose strength is in the Lord, whose hearts are set on pilgrimage. As they pass through the Valley of Baka, they make it a place of springs." Psalm 84:5–6

"He gives strength to the weary and increases the power of the weak. Isaiah 40:29

"For I can do all this through him who gives me strength." Philippians 4:13

"...suffering produces perseverance; perseverance, character; and character hope." Romans 5:3-4

"...because we know that the testing of your faith produces perseverance." James1:3

Devotional

You have carried this a long time. You have brought it to God again and again. Your tears became part of your prayer. Still, you keep walking and you feel tired. Waiting is not a passive place. It is a journey of faith. Some days feel like mountains; other days feel like valleys. Some days you dance; other days you drag your feet. Either way, you are still on the road, and every step counts.

This journey is forming you. Strength is rising within you, strength that holds both joy and trust in the middle of hardship. You don't have to pretend everything is fine. You are allowed to feel the weight of the road. You are not walking it alone. God strengthens you as you go.

The psalmist says, "Blessed are those whose strength is in the Lord, whose hearts are set on pilgrimage." That pilgrimage speaks of a long journey with sacred purpose. It is not about speed or ease. It is about direction. Your steps matter because you know Who walks with you.

Psalm 84 describes a valley called Baka, a place of sorrow and dryness. It does not say you get to skip that valley. It says you pass through it. And when you do, something happens. The place of weeping becomes a place of springs. Tears begin to water new life. God uses what broke you to strengthen you, allowing joy to grow.

Strength in waiting is not about struggling your way through without peace. It is about learning to draw daily from the Lord's presence. Romans 5 reminds us the suffering produces perseverance which builds our character and hope. James 1 tells us that the testing of our faith produces perseverance, so that we may be mature and complete. Strength is not forged in comfort but in the pressing, in the long journey where God teaches us to rely fully on Him.

That kind of strength does not rise from within. It flows from Him. "Blessed are those whose strength is in the Lord," the psalm says. We are not sustained by our attempts to make everything right on our own. Strength for the journey forms in a heart that seeks His presence more than it seeks an outcome.

Isaiah 40:31 gives us a promise to cling to: "Those who wait on the Lord will renew their strength. They will soar on wings like eagles; they will run and not grow weary; they will walk and not faint." Waiting on the Lord is not weakness. It is renewal. God infuses His strength into weary hearts, lifting them higher than they could ever go on their own.

Philippians 4:13 confirms this: "I can do all this through Him who gives me strength." The strength we need does not come from our own determination but from God, who dwells within us. Christ supplies what we lack, carrying us forward when our own reserves run dry.

His Voice in the Waiting

I see you walking when the road feels long. I know the weight you carry and the questions that circle in your mind. You are not on this journey alone. I walk with you, step by step, and nothing in your journey is wasted. I strengthen you when you feel empty. I steady you when hope trembles. Keep your eyes on Me. Stay near Me. I am here. I am faithful. I will carry you forward.

Faith in Motion

Write the word "pilgrimage" at the top of a journal page.

Beneath it, reflect on your walk with God in this waiting season:

- Who am I becoming as I wait?
- What truth will I hold on to today?
- What posture will I choose as I go forward?

Then declare:

"I am on a pilgrimage. I will walk with God through every valley. He is my strength for the journey."

Scripture in Action

Choose one of today's verses and carry it with you.

Write it on a card or in your phone.

When you feel weary or discouraged, speak it aloud.

- "Blessed are those whose strength is in the Lord, whose hearts are set on pilgrimage. As they pass through the Valley of Baka, they make it a place of springs." — Psalm 84:5–6
- "He gives strength to the weary and increases the power of the weak. Isaiah 40:29
- "For I can do all this through him who gives me strength." Philippians 4:13

Let the Word shape your steps today. Remember He is with you through it all.

Pause + Ponder

- What has this valley taught you about who God is?

- What have you learned about yourself on this journey?

- How has your understanding of strength changed as you wait?

- Where has gratitude changed your perspective in a hard season?

- Which memory of God's past faithfulness gives you courage today?

- Who in your community strengthens your faith when you feel weak?

Joy Spark

Where in your journey have you seen a glimpse of beauty or wonder?

Look for one moment today where hope flickers or peace surprises your heart.

Pay attention.

Joy often rises along the path, like a spring in the valley.

Closing Prayer

Lord, my strength is in you.

Set my heart on pilgrimage so that even in valleys I will find springs of life.

Teach me to lean on prayer, to be renewed by Your Word, to live

with gratitude.

Teach me worship even in weakness.

Remind me of Your faithfulness, and surround me with people who

encourage my walk.

Turn my tears into refreshment, my weakness into strength,

my steps into worship.

You are my strength for the journey, and I will trust you every step of the way.

In Jesus' Name,

Amen.

Remembering who God is becomes the doorway to renewed hope.

Notes

Worship for the Journey

When words fall short, worship helps carry us forward. These songs are prayers and reminders that God is near in the waiting, in the silence, and in the ache. As you walk through this devotional, let these songs walk with you. Play them in your car, in your home, or in the quiet before bed. Let them remind you that you are not alone.

Day 1: Breaking Through

Breakthrough — Red Rocks Worship
Do It Again — Elevation Worship

Day 2: The Ache of Unanswered Prayer

Even in the Silence — JWLKRS Worship
While I Wait — Lincoln Brewster

Day 3: When Striving Ceases

Nothing Else — Cody Carnes
Trust in You — Lauren Daigle

Day 4: Where Faith Keeps Knocking

Way Maker — Leeland
Promises — Maverick City Music

Day 5: Choosing Joy in the Waiting

Joy in the Morning — Tauren Wells
House of the Lord — Phil Wickham

Day 6: Learning to Hope Again

Take Courage — Kristene DiMarco
Praise Your Name — Cory Voss

Day 7: Strength for the Journey

Even If — MercyMe
Oceans (Where Feet May Fail) — Hillsong UNITED

Tools for the Journey

So how do we walk in that strength when the journey feels long? Scripture points us to practical rhythms that build courage and endurance:

Prayer: Strength grows as we stay in constant conversation with God. Prayer is not a last resort but the daily breath that keeps us connected to His power. When we pour out our hearts before Him, He exchanges our weakness for His strength. Every whispered prayer, even when words feel few, becomes an anchor that holds us steady.

God's Word: Meditating on Scripture renews our minds and strengthens our hearts. Every promise we store up becomes a well we can draw from in dry seasons. God's Word reminds us who He is and who we are in Him, steadying us when doubts rise. The more we root ourselves in truth, the less room fear and worry have to grow.

Gratitude: Practicing gratitude in hardship shifts our focus from worry to worship. A grateful heart acknowledges God's goodness even when circumstances have not yet changed. Gratitude turns our eyes from what is missing to what has already been given. Even a small list of blessings written in a journal can reframe a weary day and restore joy. One way to nurture gratitude is to walk through life looking for wonder. God often reveals Himself in the smallest places, a wildflower sprouting between cracks, the colors of a sunset, or the majesty of a mountain. These glimpses remind us that His beauty and care surround us, even in hard seasons.

Worship: Singing truth when your heart feels heavy is an act of faith. Worship through song lifts our perspective and reminds us that God is greater than our valley. Music has a way of reaching places words cannot, softening our hearts and strengthening our hope. Worship is not only a response to God's goodness; it is also a pathway back to joy.

Remembering: Strength rises when we remember God's past faithfulness. Looking back at how He has carried us before gives confidence that He will do it again. Testimonies of God's provision, healing, or guidance remind us that He is still the same today. Memory fuels endurance by pointing us to a God who never changes.

Purpose in Hardship: Accepting that God shapes us through the hard places reframes our struggle. Strength forms when we see hardship not as wasted pain but as a refining fire. Every trial has the potential to deepen our faith and prepare us for what lies ahead. When we view difficulty through the lens of God's purpose, courage begins to grow.

Community: God strengthens us through the encouragement and prayers of others. We were never meant to walk the journey alone. A trusted friend's prayer or a word of encouragement can remind us that God has not forgotten us. Community lifts our burdens when they feel too heavy to carry alone, showing us God's love in tangible ways.

These practices don't erase the valley, but they give us the tools to walk through it with courage and joy.

Continuing the Journey

The journey doesn't end here; joy is meant to be lived, shared, and renewed each day.

Visit https://thejoypursuitjourney.com for more devotionals, Joy Sparks, and free resources to help you keep growing in joy and faith.

You can also connect with me on Instagram at **@famiagreen** for encouragement, behind-the-scenes inspiration, and new releases.

Want to go deeper? Subscribe to receive *What It Means to Be a Joy Warrior*, a free guide designed to help you learn to fight for joy and live it out every day.

A Note of Thanks

Thank you for walking through these pages with me. My prayer is that even in the silence, you've discovered that God is nearer than you imagined and that joy can still bloom in the waiting.

To every friend, family member, and reader who believed in this message, your encouragement helped bring it to life.

"You make known to me the path of life; you will fill me with joy in your presence, with eternal pleasures at your right hand." **Psalm 16:11**

May His joy continue to fill you.

Famia

www.ingramcontent.com/pod-product-compliance
Lightning Source LLC
Chambersburg PA
CBHW051737040426
42447CB00008B/1182